POWER UP

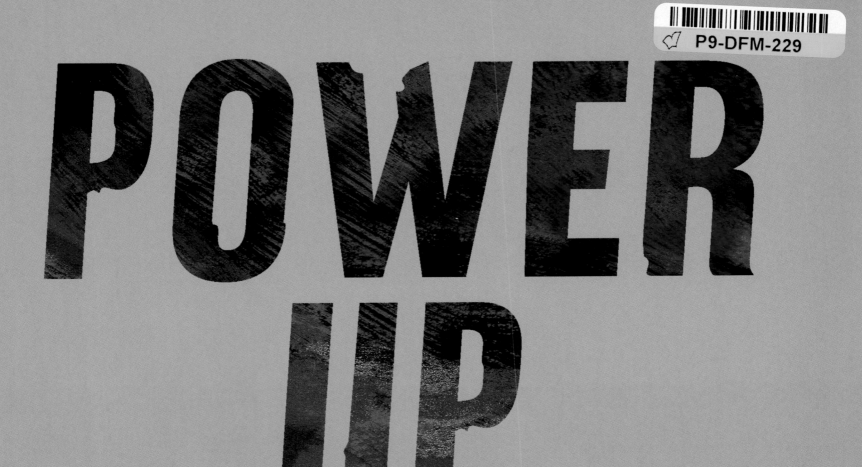

BY Seth Fishman

ILLUSTRATED BY Isabel Greenberg

Greenwillow Books
An Imprint of HarperCollinsPublishers

Power Up
Text copyright © 2019 by Seth Fishman
Illustrations copyright © 2019 by Isabel Greenberg
All rights reserved. Manufactured in China.
For information address HarperCollins Children's Books,
a division of HarperCollins Publishers,
195 Broadway, New York, NY 10007.
www.harpercollinschildrens.com

The full-color art was prepared digitally.
The text type is 20-point Abadi MT.

Library of Congress Cataloging-in-Publication Data

Names: Fishman, Seth, author. |
Greenberg, Isabel, illustrator.
Title: Power up / written by Seth Fishman ;
illustrated by Isabel Greenberg.
Description: First edition. | New York, NY : Greenwillow
Books, an imprint of HarperCollins Publishers, [2019] |
Audience: Ages 4–8. | Audience: K to grade 3.
Identifiers: LCCN 2018015694 |
ISBN 9780062455796 (hardcover)
Subjects: LCSH: Human physiology—Juvenile literature. |
Human body—Juvenile
literature. | Metabolism—Juvenile literature.
Classification: LCC QM27 .F57 2019 | DDC 612—dc23
LC record available at https://lccn.loc.gov/2018015694

19 20 21 22 23 SCP 10 9 8 7 6 5 4 3 2 1
First Edition

GREENWILLOW BOOKS

For my pop, where my science brain came from—S. F.

Do you want to hear something incredible?
You are a fireball.

No, really.

You are a walking,

breathing,

laughing,

singing

SHINING STAR

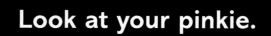

That little finger has enough energy to light up one of the biggest cities in the world for an entire day. That's power for

four million refrigerators,

seven million TVs,

eighteen hundred schools,

and about twelve thousand stoplights.

So why can't you just power your toys
or night-lights or games as if you were a battery?

Because you can't flip a switch and turn your pinkie power on and off. And that's a good thing . . .

because your body needs all the energy it's got.

Because everything you do—
even if you don't know you're doing it—
takes energy.

Just READING THIS PAGE requires ENERGY because your eyes are absorbing light beams, kind of like backward lasers!

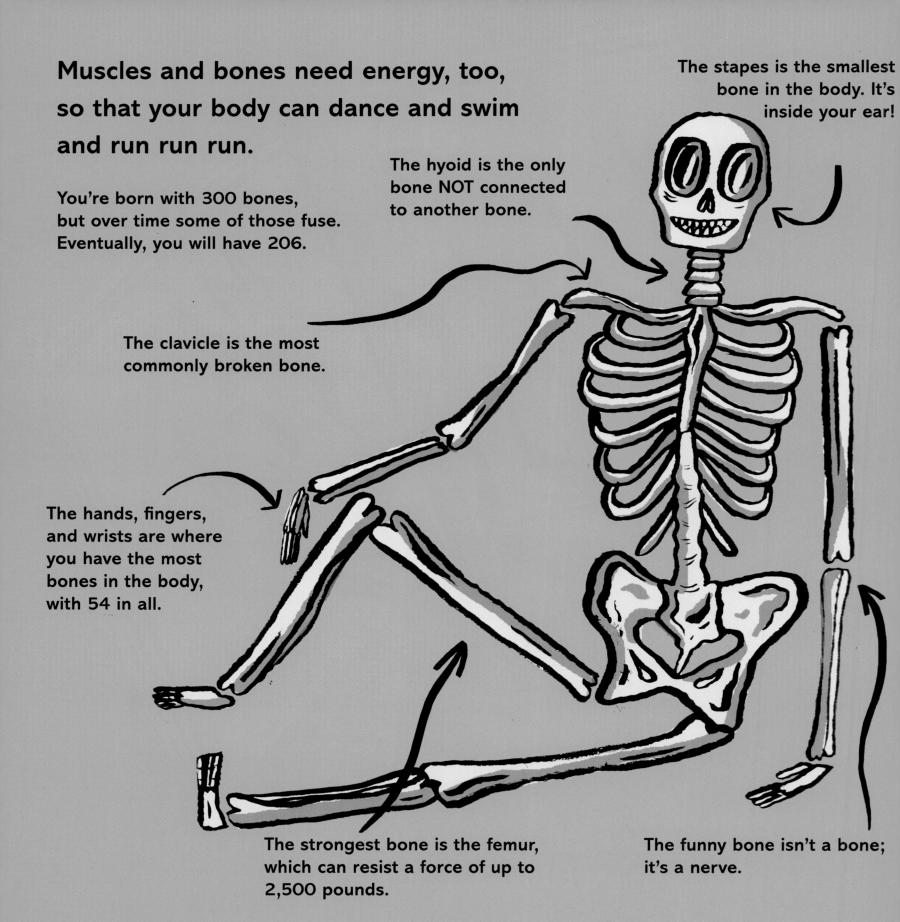

Muscles and bones need energy, too, so that your body can dance and swim and run run run.

You're born with 300 bones, but over time some of those fuse. Eventually, you will have 206.

The stapes is the smallest bone in the body. It's inside your ear!

The hyoid is the only bone NOT connected to another bone.

The clavicle is the most commonly broken bone.

The hands, fingers, and wrists are where you have the most bones in the body, with 54 in all.

The strongest bone is the femur, which can resist a force of up to 2,500 pounds.

The funny bone isn't a bone; it's a nerve.

You have at least 640 muscles and might even have as many as 850.
(Scientists are still arguing about what should be called a muscle.)

The stapedius is the smallest muscle. It's inside your ear!

The jaw muscle is, arguably, the strongest in your body.

Your heart is a muscle. It pumps about 1,500 gallons of blood a day!

Your digestive muscles help you throw up when you're sick. Yay?

The calf has seven muscles. They help you point your toes.

The gluteus maximus is the largest muscle.

And boy can you *run*.

Even the cheetah, the fastest mammal on Earth,
can only maintain bursts of speed for a short distance.

But a human once ran 310 miles
in three days *without stopping.*

Why bother stopping when you can keep running,
playing instruments, building cities, baking cakes,
and searching the sky for other planets
like Earth?

The thing is, we have to stop at some point.
Our bodies need to rest and recharge.

HOW TO RECHARGE YOUR BODY

EAT   SLEEP

A recharged body means a well-fed brain,

which is the true super power inside you.

Fast, witty, and brilliant, your brain is a

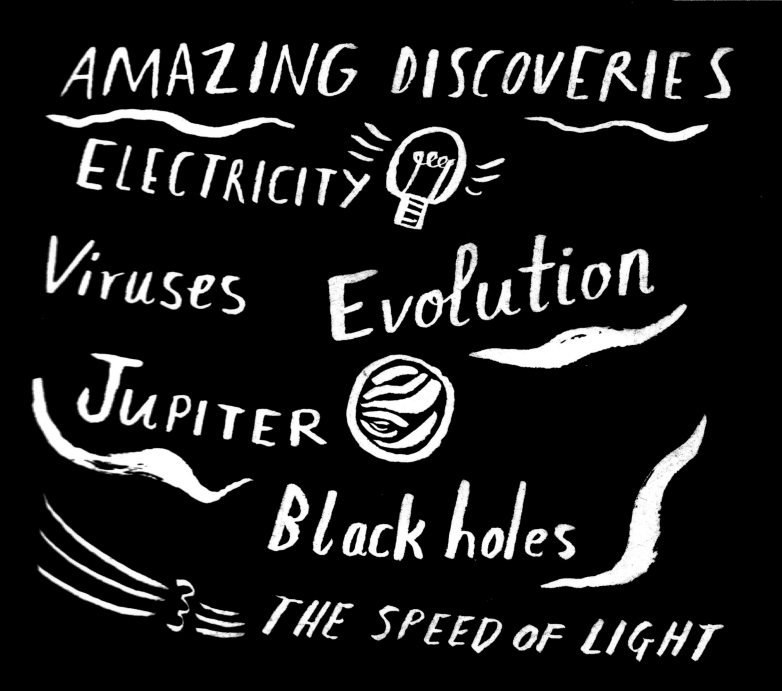

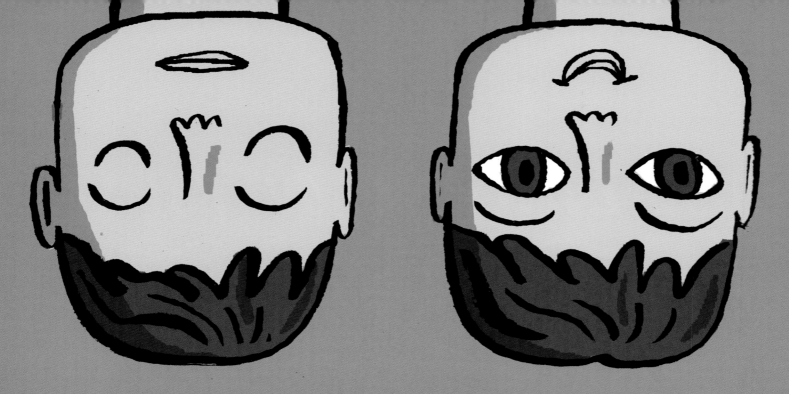

Every day, while you are blinking
15,000 times,

walking 10,000 steps,

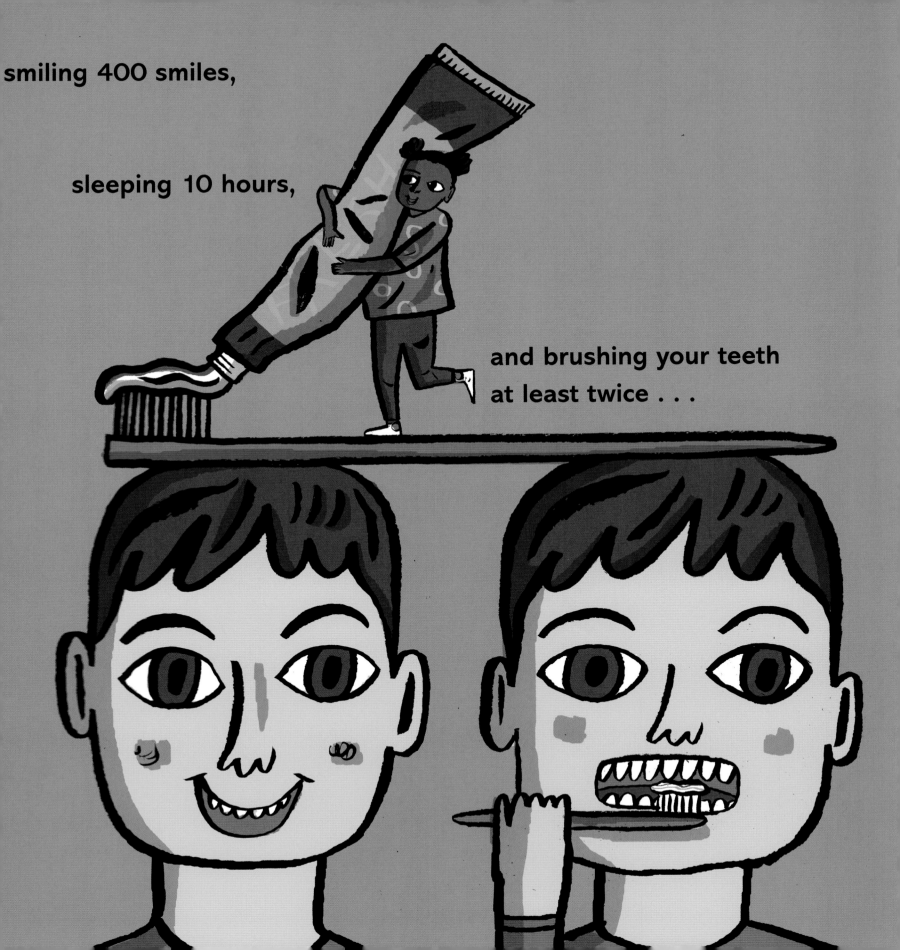

your brain is expanding and growing and putting two and two together. And whatever you did (or will do) today will help you discover or invent the next great thing.

2 + 2 =

Remember, your mind and your body are hungry for energy.

You need to feed them books,

eat broccoli,

stare at the stars,

run in place,

share with friends,

Author's Note

Is it true? Is your body really full of energy, just like a star? Yes, it is! Let me explain a little bit about how we know that.

A very famous and important equation is hidden in this book. Maybe you spotted it on the chalkboard: $E=mc^2$. What does $E=mc^2$ mean? What do those letters stand for? What is an equation?

An equation is like a sentence, but instead of words it has numbers, letters, and symbols. The = symbol is called an equal sign. It means that everything on one side of the = is the same as everything on the other. Two hippos plus two hippos is the same as four hippos. Or, 2+2=4.

$E=mc^2$ is an equation, too. But it is more complicated than 2+2=4. Understanding it takes years of work and study. The $E=mc^2$ equation was formulated by a scientist named Albert Einstein. Einstein was a whiz at math who excelled at solving very difficult problems. He liked to create imaginary scenarios to help him uncover answers, like what would happen if you were in an elevator in outer space. Einstein's curiosity and imagination led him to discover so many important things that today people will call you an "Einstein" if they think you are really smart!

In this equation, the E stands for *energy*. Energy is the ability to do work. It exists all around us, in all kinds of forms. You saw some of them in this book: running, reading, playing instruments, and more.

The m stands for *mass*. Mass is the amount of matter, or physical stuff, in an object.

The c stands for the *speed of light*. Do you remember seeing that on the chalkboard, too? The speed of light is a very, very big number: 299,792,458 meters per second. It takes light only eight minutes to travel from the sun to the earth, a distance of around 93 million miles. By comparison, a car driving that distance, going the speed limit on a highway nonstop, would take more than 163 *years* to get to the sun.

And what about that little 2 above the c? That says to square the number that it is attached to, which means to multiply it by itself—the square of 3 is 3x3=9. In other words, c^2 takes an already *huge* number (the speed of light) and makes it MUCH bigger.

So the $E=mc^2$ equation says energy is equal to mass times the speed of light squared. Something very small, with a little bit of mass—like your pinkie finger— has a huge amount of energy inside it. Ever since scientists figured out that $E=mc^2$, they have been researching all sorts of ways to get as much energy out of little things as possible. That includes splitting apart or fusing together atoms, which is called nuclear power.

Now think about how big you are compared to your pinkie. Or how big your parents are. Your bed, a car, a house, a building, a *mountain*. The world is full of energy sitting right underneath the surface, ready to burst into action.

Remember, Einstein used the energy in his brain to discover $E=mc^2$. And others have used their brains to discover what viruses are, or that Jupiter is a planet and not a star in the sky, or that there's a black hole in the center of our galaxy.

Now's your chance. Go eat some growing food, rest, work out that pinkie, keep asking "What if?" and "Why?" and put something new up on that chalkboard of human discoveries and accomplishments.